COLOR YOURSELF INSPIRED

EVERYDAY

Encouragement

Coloring Book

SPIRITUAL REFRESHMENT FOR WOMEN

Cover illustration: Katie Wood
Interior illustrations: Hannah Marks, Emma Segal, Katie Wood

Published by Barbour Books, an imprint of Barbour Publishing, Inc., P.O. Box 719, Uhrichsville, OH 44683, www.barbourbooks.com

Our mission is to publish and distribute inspirational products offering exceptional value and biblical encouragement to the masses.

Member of the
Evangelical Christian
Publishers Association

Printed in the United States of America.

COLOR YOURSELF INSPIRED

EVERYDAY

Encouragement

Coloring Book

SPIRITUAL REFRESHMENT FOR WOMEN

BARBOUR BOOKS

An Imprint of Barbour Publishing, Inc.

GIVE THANKS TO
GOD
AS YOU ASK
HIM
FOR WHAT YOU
NEED.

Philippians 4:6

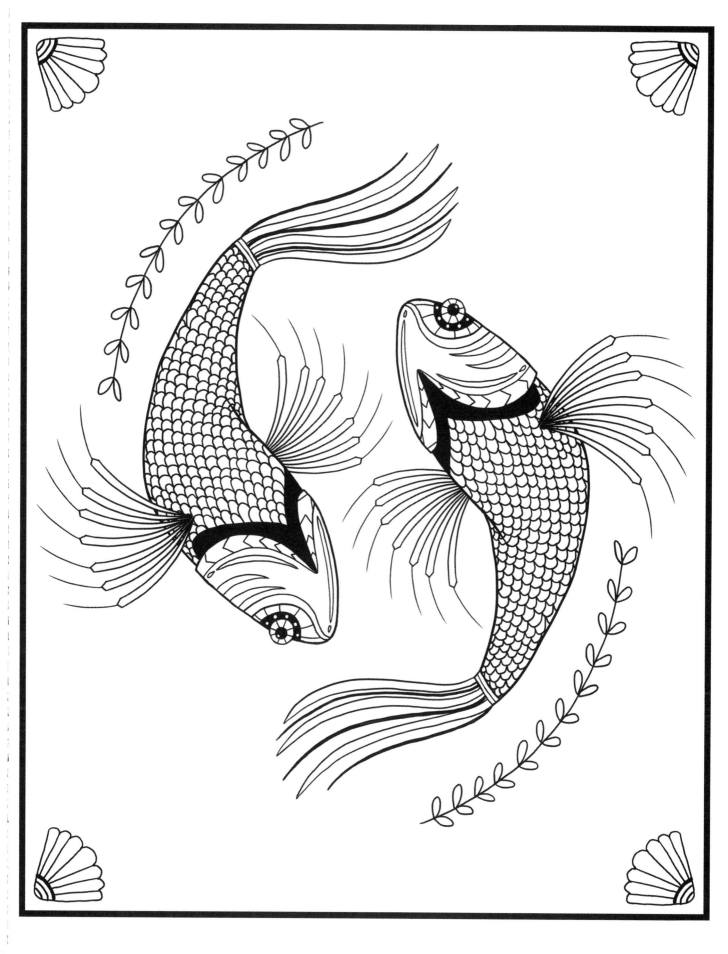

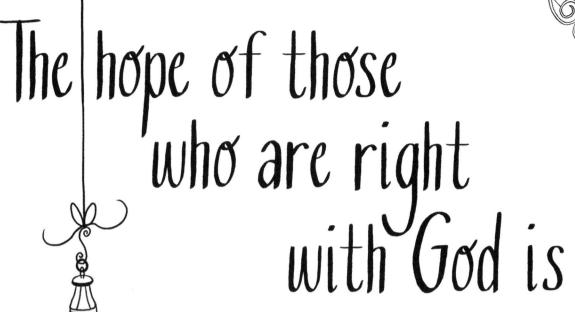

The hope of those who are right with God is JOY.

PROVERBS 10:28

DRAW EVER NEARER TO THE HEAVENLY

CREATOR;

SEEK TO DO HIS WILL.

But as for me, it is good to be near God. I have made the Lord God my safe place.

PSALM 73:28

Comfort is
a heavenly
blessing.

WHEN MY WORRY IS GREAT WITHIN ME,

YOUR

COMFORT

BRINGS

JOY

TO MY

SOUL.

PSALM 94:19

Look to the Shepherd for peace.

PLACE YOUR TRUST IN HIM,
WHO LOVED YOU FROM THE START.

I trust in you,

O LORD.

I say,

"you are my

GOD"

PSALM 31:14

Let us keep looking to Jesus.

HEBREWS 12:2

Rejoice in the Savior's deep love for you.

I PRAY that you will be able to UNDERSTAND how wide & how long & how high & how deep His love is.

Ephesians 3:18

"Give and it will be given to you. You will have more than enough."

LUKE 6:38

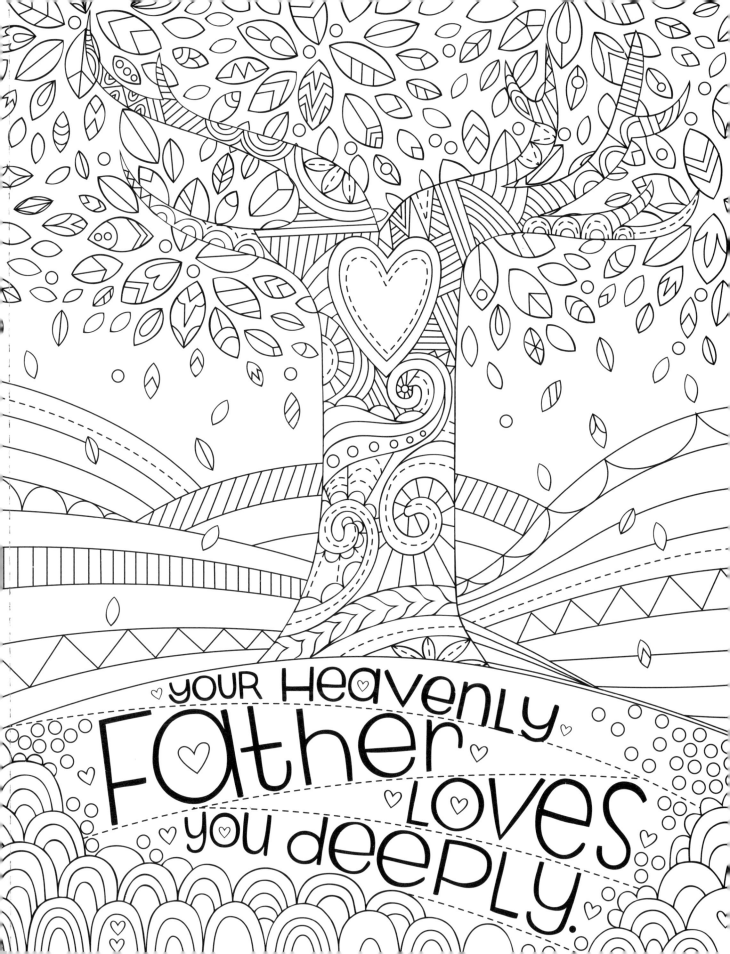

"For God so loved
the world that He gave
His only Son.
Whoever puts his
trust in God's Son will
not be lost but will
have life that lasts

FOREVER."

JOHN 3:16

With JESUS in your HEART, you always have a PEACEFUL PLACE to GO.

Her Ways ARE pleasing, AND ALL her PATHS are peace

PROVERBS 3:17

GOD has said, "I will never leave you or let you be alone."

HEBREWS 13:5

GOD MAKES all THINGS Work TOGETHER for THE GOOD of THOSE WHO love HIM and are CHOSEN to be a part of HIS PLAN.

ROMANS 8:28